My Nature Journal

Books by Merridy Cox as editor

Annotated Edwardian Pets and How to Keep Them, by Frank Finn, 1907 (e-book)

Themes from *A Course in Miracles*: How Brothers Can Get Along

Books by Merridy Cox as author

A Swan Family's Summer (future)

The Story of Linnaeus and Binomial Nomenclature

Nature Breaks for Busy Urbanites: Five Doses for Relaxation

Fifty Shapes of Swan: A Natural History in Photos (e-book)

English Manual: Letter by Letter (excerpts in blog posts)

My Nature Journal

Merridy Cox

Lyrical Leaf Publishing

Toronto

Excerpts of text and photos from *A Swan Family's Summer*, a book of nature photography and poetry © Merridy Cox.

Nature—Animals—Birds—Mute Swans

Journal—Blank book

Environment

ISBN: 978-0-9948481-5-4

Lyrical Leaf Publishing

Toronto, Canada

www.LyricalLeafPublishing.com

My Nature Journal

Introduction

My Nature Journal may help you to write down your impressions as the seasons unfold around you, week by week, throughout the year. Include some drawings, if you wish.

Throughout history, swans symbolize grace, purity, strength and love. Perhaps the life story of Mute Swans will inspire you to look at all birds in a different light, as a way to measure the passage of time in the way that nature unfolds, one season into the next.

Swans are graceful, gliding serenely on the water near the shore. About the size of an average family dog, swans are very relatable. Mute Swans are sometimes called tame swans, because they build their nests near human activity and accept handouts for lunch.

Spending time in nature relaxes the spirit and allows the mind and body to rest and heal. To pay attention to even the smallest of details in the natural world is to find the ongoing miracles of life that are a part of the larger whole.

We are a part of nature. We have a relationship with the landscape, weather, plants and animals. They sustain us, feed us, keep us healthy and fit. It is important not to forget that our lives depend upon the rich quality of nature.

When you write your observations of nature in this journal, you create a journal of gratitude for the world around you. Share your observations with your friends. They will start to look at nature with new eyes.

—Merridy Cox

January

February

March

March, Week One

The swans have arrived:
snow, sleet, cold winds, sunny heat
matter not—it's time.

March, Week Two

The waves come and go
owning nothing—just being.
The swans wait to hear

Spring Equinox

March, Week Three

The swans recognize
their place, their community,
both diverse and safe.

March, Week Four

But, time is limited...
They search for material,
build a sturdy nest.

April

April, Week One

Here, their lives can be
fulfilled and full of promise.
Now is the swans' time.

April, Week Two

The nest is their place
of refuge and their centre
of family life.

April, Week Three

They begin to build.
The cob pulls reeds and rushes,
brings them to the nest.

April, Week Four

Anticipating
a clutch of eggs and a raft
of cygnet children.

May

May, Week One

So vulnerable
the nest—open to attack—
it is their home base.

May, Week Two

The swans know the care
that their eggs and cygnets need—
their parents taught them.

May, Week Three

The cob swan pulls reeds
as his best contribution
to the pen swan's work.

May, Week Four

The swans, cob and pen,
centre here their compassion,
their caring, their hope.

June

June, Week One

The eggs are hatching!
The cygnets enter the pond,
soon ready to swim.

June, Week Two

Their mother gives them
encouragement and watches
each and every one.

Summer Solstice

June, Week Three

The father cob swan
fulfils serious duties:
he guards his family.

June, Week Four

The height of his wings
shows his level of concern.
He makes himself big.

July

July, Week One

The downy cygnets
listen for their mother's call
to know all is well.

July, Week Two

We can't tell them, one
from one, but a mother knows.
She values each one.

July, Week Three

The family group
knows that together they're safe
cob, pen and cygnets.

July, Week Four

A mute swan's diet
is all vegetarian—
pond weed, grass, willow.

August

August, Week One

They keep to places
where there is an abundance
of green food to eat.

August, Week Two

Here is the question:
can we learn to know and love
the birds around us?

August, Week Three

It's a start for us
to know each swan as a friend,
to recognize them.

August, Week Four

The young swans, growing,
by August's end the same size
as their mother pen.

September

September, Week One

The pen on her nest
spends time preening her feathers,
each one waterproofed.

September, Week Two

A great blue heron
stabs a fish, good for dinner,
from along the shore.

Fall Equinox

September, Week Three

Pond community—
tern, robin and kingfisher—
all part of the whole.

September, Week Four

The cygnets, now grown,
start to explore on their own,
heading out further.

October

October, Week One

The pen and cob swan
loosen ties to the cygnets
as they swim further.

October, Week Two

The cob swans' black knob
is generally bigger,
the pen swans', smaller.

October, Week Three

Cygnets have pale bills
and tiny knobs that will not grow
until the next year.

October, Week Four

When all is quiet,
the cob preens all his feathers,
even those underneath.

November

November, Week One

Mute swans together
as a pair, mated for life,
know one another.

November, Week Two

Perhaps if we take
time to know them, to listen,
they will speak to us—

November, Week Three

Our mute swans do not
migrate—they don't know the place
or how to get there.

November, Week Four

It's possible that
one time soon, the geese will teach
the swans to migrate.

December

December, Week One

The swan pair, together,
spend time in sheltered water
not prone to freezing

December, Week Two

Cygnets join a band
of other young birds and geese
exploring the shores.

Winter Solstice

December, Week Three

Winter on the lake
with ducks and geese, they survived—
last year's young matured.

December, Week Four

Perhaps the cygnets
find a mate in these cold days,
waiting for the spring.

January

In January
the swans meet some northern ducks,
south from the Arctic.